I0453877

# Being the Light

## *Everyday Meditation Enlightenment*

By

*Dr. Jeanne King, Ph.D.*

**Copyright © 2025 Dr. Jeanne King, Ph.D.**
All rights reserved.

Library of Congress Control Number: 2025914928

Black-and-white ISBN: 979-8-9917619-1-8
Color ISBN: 979-8-9917619-0-1
eBook ISBN: 979-8-9917619-2-5

No part of this book may be reproduced, distributed, transmitted, or stored in any form or by any means—electronic, mechanical, photocopying, recording, or retrieval systems—without prior written permission from the author, except as permitted by U.S. copyright law.

Published in the United States by Partners in Prevention.

For additional resources, visit:
www.BeingtheLight.co

Printed in the United States of America.

First Edition

Dr. Jeanne King, Ph.D.

*In Honor of My Beloved Parents*

# Being the Light

# Dedication

*Being the Light* is dedicated to those
who are curious about meditation.
May it serve as an invitation to you
to step into the larger part of who you are.

Being the Light

# Disclaimer
*(for informational purposes only)*

The materials in *Being the Light* were prepared by Dr. Jeanne King, Ph.D., to share information and inspiration. They are offered for informational purposes only and are not intended as psychological advice or therapy.

The techniques and practices presented are for educational use, inviting personal reflection and awareness. They are not designed to diagnose psychological or psychiatric conditions, nor to provide treatment for any disorder.

Readers of *Being the Light* accept full responsibility for how they choose to use the content and practices described. The material is not intended to create, and its receipt does not constitute, a psychologist–patient relationship. This information is not a substitute for obtaining professional healthcare services.

Dr. Jeanne King, Ph.D.

# Acknowledgments

My deepest appreciation to all who have contributed to my integration of the practice of meditation, specifically Maharishi Mahesh Yogi and Dr. Patricia Carrington. To Dr. Les Fehmi and Dr. Eugene Gendlin for helping me understand the relevance of this essential practice to effective psychotherapy and to one's well-being.

I am also grateful to my mother Audree and maternal grandmother Mignon, who stepped on the meditation path along with me in the 70s. I still feel your presence in meditation today and recall the three of us sitting quietly back in the day.

And to my father Richard King, who imprinted me with the courage to pursue that which is meaningful and fulfilling to me. And all my patients, who gave me the opportunity to shine the light on a meditation path for their own personal growth, health and enlightenment.

All of the people acknowledged above are no longer with us in earthly form. Since their passing, they have remained in my heart and will always be the most influential people in my life.

My dearest life-long friend, Rosemary King, for your love and skilled proofing of this manuscript. To Elizabeth, whose support in the design has meant so much to me. And to David Fink for opening the door in the first place for this amazing journey that has enriched me over the last 52 years.

# Table of Contents

# Preface

L ike most memoirs, *Being the Light* was written for me. I have been called to tell my meditation story again and again. Over the years, I have shared bits and pieces with many people, yet I had always wanted to journal the evolution of meditation practice as it has been for me.

It is by far the most significant aspect of my daily routine. Whether I sit for 20 minutes, two hours, or merely have a glimpse of meditation upon awakening, the exquisite equanimity revealed in this practice is priceless. My goal is to share how an everyday person in academia came to fall in love with this esoteric experience, and how it has enhanced my well-being over the years.

Somewhere, I read that only 4% of the population meditates daily. Yet, far more have tried meditating in all sorts of ways.

If you are curious about this experience, may *Being the Light* add to your understanding of the impact of meditation on one's daily life and on one's larger life perspective. Moreover, may this inspire you toward enhancing your well-being through your own meditation practice.

The words I offer in *Being the Light* aren't just about what is said. It's about how it's held within you. How the content lives inside you as you take it in. The layout was chosen to encourage presence—a quiet attentiveness that allows the deeper meaning to unfold.

# PART ONE


The Evolution
of
My Meditation Journey

Being the Light

# Introduction

*"There is another world*
*inside this one,*
*no words can describe it."*
Rumi

Writing about spiritual experience is a lot like trying to describe an orgasm. While you may know the sensations and feelings associated with the words you choose, the reader most likely will not because the experience is beyond words.

Given this limitation, I will do my best in the passages that follow. My goal is to share with you what has been revealed to me in 52 years of daily meditation.

## Being the Light

Come with me and allow me to speak
to the part of you that knows you exist
beyond your body, your thoughts and your
emotions.

# CHAPTER ONE

# *Just Being*

*"We are stars wrapped in skin.*
*The light you are seeking has*
*always been within."*
Rumi

It all started on holiday break in New Orleans, waiting for a trolley with my old middle school boyfriend, David. As we were catching up on being "co-eds" in our respective colleges, he shared with me that he had been meditating.

Not knowing anything about meditation, I asked, "What's that?" and "Why are you doing it?"

David didn't have a lot of words to offer in reply. He simply said, "It's just being."

It was clear to me that it was something sacred to him by the way he responded. It was in his demeanor that I knew he was into something good.

That's as far as it went at that point in time... until the Transcendental Meditation (TM) people showed up on my campus the following semester.

**The Meditation Experiment**

I was somewhat of a lackey for my Experimental Psychology professor, Dr. McWherter, in my sophomore year at the University of Southwestern Louisiana. When the news came rushing through campus that this meditation group was coming around, my ears perked up because of that encounter I had with David months prior.

In all my enthusiasm to try this mysterious thing, endorsed by a trusted friend, I pitched the idea to Dr. McWherter for an experiment with us learning meditation.

He hesitated, asking why one would want to learn to meditate? Not having an answer for him, I leaned heavily on the literature circulating all over campus. Statements of testimonials and lists of benefits from improved well-being to enhanced performance mildly interested him.

In my discussions back and forth with the professor, we agreed that one of us would learn the "technique" and then teach it to the other. Now, who became the guinea-pig was to be determined by the toss of a coin.

Being the Light

# CHAPTER TWO

## Learning Meditation

*"If you find me not within you,*
*you will never find me.*
*For I have been with you*
*from the beginning."*
Rumi

You guessed it, heads I won. Little did I know how my life would change from that day on. I remember my initiation February 1972 like it was yesterday. Gathering my fresh fruit and flowers, I eagerly and openly sat with my meditation teacher as my new mantra rolled off his tongue into my being.

Following the practice as instructed, I just sat with the mantra as taught having absolutely no expectations whatsoever. Except at some point, I knew I'd have to teach Dr. McWherter.

Funny thing is that was impossible, because the experience was deeper than any words in my reach and I really didn't know what was yielding what this practice was doing to and for me.

So, I just became a student of meditation taking in whatever I needed to support my practice. I sat twice daily for at least 20 minutes and within weeks I knew something profound was happening.

**Profound Attention**

I had always been a straight A student and was accustomed to academic excellence. What was new for me, now meditating, was my increased capacity to absorb whatever was in front of me.

After meditation, I inhaled my studies and walked into each and every test owning it. My friends were taking uppers to stay awake all night studying, and I was meditating with results exceeding everyone around me.

Meditation for me was about enhanced focus and an air of delight in any material I dove into immediately after meditating. People would say, *"You're wasting time."*

But I knew I was clearing the deck so I could plow through with greater comprehension and retention. Meditation became my secret to academic success beyond my imagination.

I was not new to academic excellence, having spent the fourth through twelfth grade in a school for gifted children. Entry into this school required an IQ north of 164. I was a Latin scholar throughout high school, winning state rallies year after year.

I graduated valedictorian from this school, so you would think studying was no big deal for me. But meditation opened a door to learning in a way that is beyond words. Suffice it to say, I loved learning following meditation and it made me high—really high.

**Residence Courses**

During my junior and senior years of undergraduate study, I spent many long weekends in what we called "residence courses" back in the day. I remember the smell of the shared blankets encircling the meditation hall. Practicing together yielded an even more profound experience.

Many hours were spent in deep silence and viewing Maharishi Mahesh Yogi speaking around the world. His words pierced through me as he described *transcendence*. He was putting words to my experience, which carried it further.

I recall thinking and saying that what I experienced in mediation people were paying lots of money for on the streets. I was onto and into a natural high.

Holiness Maharishi Mahesh Yogi

Maharishi Mahesh Yogi Inaugurates
1st Celebration of the Age of Enlightenment

# CHAPTER THREE

# *Sitting with Chicago Police*

*"Your heart knows the way.*
*Run in that direction."*
Rumi

F ast forward a few years, I entered into Northwestern University graduate school where I earned my doctorate. I was so intrigued by the practice of meditation that I decided to create a doctoral program around learning as much as I could about meditation as it relates to well-being.

Now mind you, I am a Northwestern University graduate student studying psychology, and the subject of meditation is woo-woo in ivy league schools.

Nonetheless, I was determined. I figured if I'm going to invest two solid years of my life on a doctoral dissertation, it better be something I'm jazzed about.

**The Doctoral Committee Agreement**

So, picture this: here I am in a conference room with six professors who represented my doctoral committee. These are the people assigned to monitor, coach and assess my progress during the doctoral research.

It all started with my efforts to pitch what I sought to study. I babbled in circles talking about "centering," "stress reduction" and the like. The more I spoke, the more boring I became. I was afraid to let them know what I really wanted to study, because I thought it wouldn't be an acceptable topic for a Northwestern psychology doctoral student.

Suddenly something deep within me quietly said to me, "Tell it like it is, Jeanne." And then an abrupt about turn occurred in my rhetoric and the word "meditation" poured out along with an exhilaration that lifted my energy through the roof.

One professor said, "I don't know what the hell you are talking about, but that is what you should be studying." He happened to be the head of the School of Education, at a time heavily influenced by Dr. Carl Rogers. He was known as the student-centered professor.

Another professor said, "You should be in the School of Theology." I thought to myself, while that may be true, I don't want to start over as I had already invested four years in undergraduate psychology, two years obtaining a masters in interpersonal communication and a year plus in all of the required psychology courses to fulfill my doctorate. I was two years from the finish line and I wanted closure.

### The Psychology Experiment Promise

In all my resourcefulness, I dipped deep within and made this offer. I boldly claimed my intention of what I wanted to learn and proposed the following.

I said, I want to explore the psycho-physiology of meditation and its implications for psychotherapy. I explained, I will find a measure of successful psychotherapeutic progress and conduct an experimental study to determine if the practice of mediation impacts this measure.

I offered to do the study in an extremely rigors fashion using subjects in a professional manner without any background in meditation or bias toward becoming a meditator. I told them that I'd collect the pre and post data, teach the subjects how to meditate, do a statistical analysis of the data, and if the results were statistically significant, I would then—if they wished—write it up as my doctoral dissertation.

And they all said, "Go for it. Do it." And so, it was…

### The Chicago Police Peace Within

Having promised to make this a rigorous study, I reached out to the Chicago police. I figured if the meditation could work for them, it would generalize to other people.

I secured nearly 100 police officers volunteering for the study.

Dr. Eugene Gendlin's Experiential Focusing procedure was used to measure psychotherapy efficacy and Dr. Patricia Carrington's Clinically Standardized Meditation (CSM) protocol was used to teach meditation. CSM is a mantra meditation instruction drawing from Transcendental Meditation.

I remember moments of my teaching these police officers how to meditate like it was yesterday…even though I'm reflecting on events 47 years ago. About a week after the individual instruction, I met with the police subjects in small groups for follow-up practice and additional instruction.

Sitting in a conference room on the Evanston campus with about ten officers, we gathered around a large table upon which some officers placed their guns. I provided a guided meditation checking exercise that contained a 15-minute silence. There I sat with these men, many twice my size, eyes closed in silence. I could see shoulders relaxing, breathing deepening and an air of peacefulness in faces. It was utterly magnificent.

Peeking out of the corner of my closed eyes, I saw a blasting light from the sun hitting one of the guns placed on the table. The juxtaposition of the peace in this one officer's face and the image of the gun glistering was ever so striking. I'll never forget it.

As I went around the room checking in with those wishing to speak, this one officer subject said, "Never in my life have I ever felt tranquility as I just experienced."

His words pierced my being, and that day became the beginning of a 25-year practice, teaching psychotherapy patients how to meditate. These police officers taught me how to relay the esoteric concepts of meditation into everyday nuts and bolts language of the everyday person.

We gave each other precious gifts. That experience was the foundation of an affinity I developed for law enforcement. In fact, one of my first patients in my private practice was a police chief with a stress-related gastro-intestinal disorder. I still have the wooden clock he made for me after a very successful treatment intervention.

Dr. Jeanne King, Ph.D.

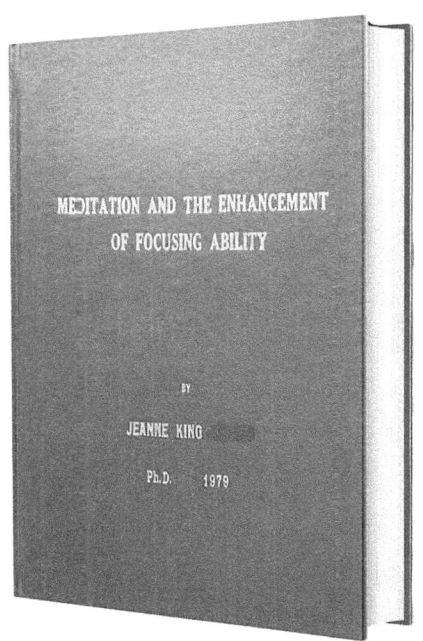

*Meditation and the Enhancement
of Focusing Ability*
Dr. Jeanne King, PhD.

Doctoral Dissertation 1979
Northwestern University          .

# Being the Light

# CHAPTER FOUR

## *Kissing God*

*I asked God,*
*"Do not let me die until I know you."*
*God replied,*
*"He who knows Me never dies."*
Rumi

When I entered into graduate school for my doctorate, I was two years into a marriage with my first husband Joe (his name changed for the sake of this writing). He was a peaceful man with his own baggage. The lifestyle he led drove me to divorce, because it conflicted with what marriage meant to me. I trust you can read between the lines here.

During the years we were together, he practiced his version of meditation (lots of television) and I practiced mine. His admired younger brother was also a TM meditation practitioner. I assumed this made my practice acceptable.

Back in those days, before I discovered the cushion, I meditated in comfortable chairs. We had this classic traditional winged back chair in our bedroom where I did my daily mediations.

My routine was to sit in the morning after Joe left for work and again late afternoon following a full day of classes or study. The meditations during this period of time in my life, in which I was studying and teaching meditation, were extremely profound.

I recall dipping into stillness that locked me into bliss beyond words. I used to refer to the experience as *"kissing God."* The experience was ever so magnificent. And it happened again and again, more often than not.

One day I recall sitting on our bed with Joe and opening up about these experiences. I told him these words, "It doesn't matter if I die, because I have lived as much as anyone could ever desire." I said, "I am complete."

I was not in any way suicidal. To the contrary, I was full of life embracing my blessings. I was so over the top with fullness, I needed—nor did I want—anything further. I was fulfilled. The happiness within me was beyond words. It was truly "over the top."

Joe looked puzzled when I said this, and he paused. Then he replied, "One day you will be sitting on a mountain top somewhere." I realized he was disturbed by my comment.

*"Once the silent stillness tiptoes in,
you feel as though you are hugging God
and God is hugging you.
It's the most nourishing experience ever."*

Dr. Jeanne King, Ph.D.
(Joe's forecast 20 years later)
Sedona, AZ 2000

# Being the Light

# CHAPTER FIVE

# Applied Psychophysiology

*"A candle never loses any of its light
While lighting up another candle."*
Rumi

I opened my first office in Northbrook, Illinois in 1981, where I taught patients with stress-related illnesses how to meditate. This brought me to Biofeedback as a means to evidence to people the physiological changes taking place in relation to mental and psychological changes under their voluntary control. We called this mind-body discipline Allied Psychophysiology

During one of the many professional conferences that I attended in the early 1980's, I met a man by the name of Dr. Les Fehmi from Princeton University. Dr. Fehmi, developer of the Open Focus technique, was heavily into EEG training.

I purchased a five-channel, phase-sensitive EEG from Dr. Fehmi and became proficient in teaching EEG coherence biofeedback in my clinical practice with patients. It was extremely rewarding to witness the physical and psychological changes in my patient population.

As I deepened my understanding of teaching altered states of consciousness, my own consciousness was expanding. I clearly remember the awe I felt noticing how the equanimity of meditation carried over into activity. This carryover effect was the most stunning aspect of meditation practice during this phase of my life.

I continued this work for the next 18 years expanding my practice, as I developed. First, I moved my clinical practice to an office on Michigan Ave in downtown Chicago, and then launched the Chicago Center for the Treatment of Pain and Stress at One East Wacker. I was so proud of my clinical practice and the results we were getting over the years.

Patients were healing, and often resolving, long-standing chronic pain conditions, fibromyalgia, sleep disorders, irritable bowel syndrome, essential hypertension, depressive affective disorders and many other psychological-mental, behavioral conditions.

## Unalignment in Marriage and Meditation

When I met my second husband (whom I call Lucifer for the purpose of this writing), I played down my love for meditation and my enthusiasm around my professional accomplishments.

You might wonder, why? It was my way of keeping peace during our life together from 1983 through 1995. I remember making it just this thing I did, and this professional practice I pursued.

We decided to marry after I became pregnant in 1983 four months into our relationship. Little did I know at the time; meditation was what made it possible for me to endure his horrific psychological abuse. And in later years, it aided in my recovery from physical injuries resulting from his domestic assaults.

The full story of this relationship beginning to end can be found in *All But My Soul: Abuse Beyond Control* All But My Soul.pdf.

Suffice it to say, meditation gave me an Armor of God and served to shield me from the dreadful, routine emotional and verbal assaults I was subjected to in our home (and on exotic vacations).

**Sleep Witnessing and The Flying Block**

In 1986, I participated in the Transcendental Meditation Sidhi Program. This practice catapulted my meditation experience twenty-fold. Essentially, it put what I had been doing prior on steroids.

I'm going to write about a spiritual experience I have never written about, so hold on as I try to describe this experience. I was in Washington DC for this advanced meditation instruction. I shared a room with a roommate and can still see my bed next to the wall.

We had received the first part of the advanced instruction and retreated to our rooms for the evening. Lights were always out at 10:00 PM in all residence events. My preparations for bed and what I can recall in falling asleep were ordinary.

However, at some point in the evening, I was fully awake and asleep at the same time. I was totally and completely witnessing myself sleeping. There were blocks of dreaming which I took in as one might watch a movie. But instead of this just being mindful of dreaming during sleep, it was magnitudes more. I was in a state of profound bliss beyond any words I can find to convey it. It was magnificent, pure ecstasy… just simply witnessing sleep.

That feeling stayed with me into the next day and beyond. I met up with a colleague from the TM movement. This man was one of the lead doctorate level researchers on the psychophysiology of meditation, back in the day.

I told him what was happening to me, and he replied, "Enjoy, but don't get attached to it." He noted those experiences come and go as part of one's practice.

The years that followed, as I practiced the Sidhi program, continued to deepen my understanding and experience of meditation. All that time, I kept the depth of this experience to myself, continuing to tell my then-husband, I was just meditating. No big deal. However, I knew I was slipping into the Armor of God.

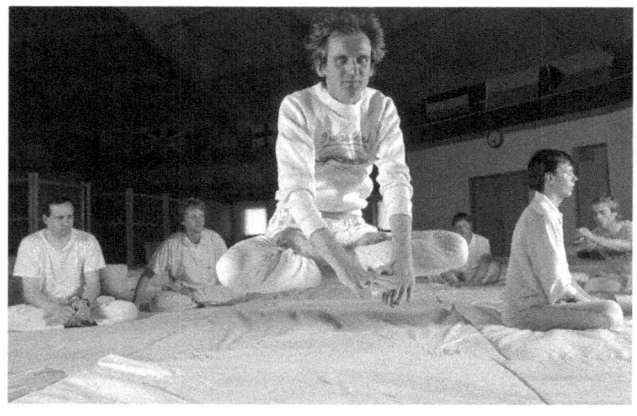

Transcendental Meditation Sidhi Program
Yogic Flying

Transcendental Meditation Sidhi Program
Yogic Flying – Men's Dome

Dr. Jeanne King, Ph.D.

Dr. Jeanne King, Ph.D.
TM Sidhi Program Dome Badge
1986 Yogic Flying Blo

35

# Being the Light

# CHAPTER SIX

## *Healing Meditation*

*"When the world pushes you to your knees,
you're in the perfect position to pray."*
Rumi

Three children were born into that conflicted marriage. After my first was nearly two, I returned to work part-time. Over the next 10 years, I maintained a part-time work schedule so I could raise my children, as they were my primary focus.

## Violence Hits Home

I remember taking the train home on my days at the office. I would finish with my last patient and then round the day out with my own meditation. Sitting on the train during the commute, I'd write thank you letters and progress notes to referring doctors.

There was something about writing following meditation that took the whole meditation carryover magnitudes beyond. Then, when I hit that door met by three bouncing boys, I was all sunshine. And we basked in that delight…until their father came home frequently tearing into me or our oldest son.

The violence in our home had become commonplace. Police were in and out more times than I could count. It was disgusting. I had sustained multiple physical injuries and so had our oldest son. As mentioned earlier, this entire story is detailed in **All But My Soul:** *Abuse Beyond Control.*

But for the sake of context, I'll mention this one episode. Our oldest who was three at the time, called out, from his crib, "one more kiss, Mommy," as he was going to sleep. I believe I was lying on the bed in our master bedroom nursing our second son.

In our first son's outcry for one more kiss Mommy, he was met with a slap on his face— leaving his father's handprint in black and blue. Mind you, this child had already sustained a dislocated arm because he was fascinated by candies in a checkout isle. I trust you get the picture and my point.

Anyway, my challenging this handling of our child resulted in me being thrown to the floor, arms stretched out resulting in a cervical spine injury that took four years to fully resolve.

In my struggle to heal and become pain free, I chatted with a dear friend who had been one of the research physicians in the TM movement. We were sitting in the biofeedback lab in my Michigan Avenue office and he said to me, "Do you want to get better?"

He said it as though I had a choice. "Absolutely," I said. And then he told me about Pancha Karma.

**Bliss Beyond…Ecstasy Everywhere**

Lucifer used to take a two-week fishing trip with his father every June. So, I decided to capitalize on his absence. It was the only time I thought I could actually get away without the roof falling in, if you know what I mean.

I made cassette tapes of me singing to our two children as they fell asleep so they'd have my voice with the click of their little fingers. I loved making these tapes for them and they loved listening to them.

I headed to Lancaster the moment Lucifer took off to Canada. He went fishing and I went healing. And boy did I heal. I headed to the TM Pancha Karma Healing Center for the cleansing of my lifetime (at least until that point in time).

Deepak Chopra was one of the primary doctors at the center during this time. It was back in the day when Deepak would spend 20-30 minutes with "the guests" one-on-one. I learned so much from him over the many years I continued to return for Pancha Karma.

Somewhere in or around the third day of this intense healing regimen, I had the breakthrough of my life. I was lying on the table receiving a PK treatment (as we affectionally called it). Two people were working on me at the same time.

As they were finishing the body treatment stroking my neck along my carotid artery, I felt myself taking a huge deep breath. On the

41

exhale an electrical pop busted out from my neck reverberating into and down the entire core of my being.

When I got up, I was pain free for the first time in many months. That experience changed me and forever changed my perspective of the body's capacity to heal itself. I was hooked! And I continued to go back year after year, for over a decade.

I can recall lying in bed the night this healing shift occurred. The stillness and silence within were palpable. It was a depth of which I had not yet tasted in all my years of meditating. I was a *lightness of being* in every step…and that joy remained with me for nearly a month.

I can remember, as though it was yesterday, how I felt upon returning to Chicago. I was happier and healthier than I had been in years. Roughly one week after my return, I was in a taxi headed down Lake Shore Drive to my Michigan Avenue office. It was the first day going back to my part-time clinical practice.

Please understand I'm not crazy as I write this, though I know it may sound nuts. The only way I can describe this to you is to say, it was like I was on ecstasy. Now, I have never taken ecstasy or any mind-altering psychedelic substances.

I use the word "ecstasy," because it so accurately describes what was within and around me in that drive down Lake Shore Drive. All I could see from both side windows in that vehicle was boundlessness. The sheer delightful expansiveness was beyond anything I had ever known.

It was as though *my consciousness was inside and outside of me at the same time.*

I was ever so keenly aware of the "inter-connectiveness" of all things… of all beings… of everything. *I was blessed in simply being.*

I was so high and so happy, I feared I'd leave my family just to have this experience forever. So, I made the decision to get pregnant again, because I couldn't be without my two sons. It was out of this extraordinary bliss that a third child was conceived.

*"When the silence within
fills every morsel of space
within and around you,
heal and enjoy."*

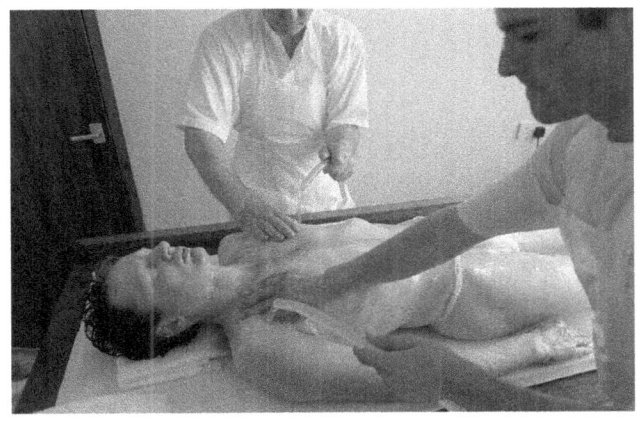

Pancha Karma Sarvangadhara Oil Massage

*"In the utter silence,*
*you are on God's operating table*
*and the cells are further apart."*

# CHAPTER SEVEN

## My Father's Passing

*"Be watchful.*
*The grace of God appears suddenly.*
*It comes without warning to an open heart."*
Rumi

In 1993, my father was diagnosed with lung cancer and everything changed. My attention shifted from the turmoil in my little family to the major upset for my parents. It was surreal and very real, all at the same time.

Dad needed to have heart surgery just to qualify for the cancer treatments to follow. All along his journey, I questioned his prescribed therapies, sometimes openly but more often privately, because I knew the path they embraced. And nothing was changing it.

The day before one of his surgeries, I sat in the hospital in a secluded area, looking out of a wide window. Simply gazing with my eyes opening and closing, I fell into a very deep mediation.

Suddenly, I felt this huge mass inside my chest, as though it was an iron ball gaining momentum to thrust out from the front of my chest. I know that sounds bizarre, but that's exactly what I felt.

When I re-entered my dad's room there was all this talk about the mass in my father's chest. I didn't say anything to anyone about what I had experienced, but I knew he was, indeed, in trouble.

It was a difficult time for all of us—my mother, my father and my broken little family. Then in December 1994, I received that call no-one wants to get. It was time to say good-by to Dad.

My father was the kindest person I have ever known. He was so good to me growing up. I loved him immensely. I remember curtseying for him when I was 10. I was his little princess and he was my forever hero.

**Eternity on Wheels**

I arrived in Palm Springs where my parents were living at the time. It was days before Dad's last breath. I remember sleeping in my parents' guest room on an air bed. We were all rushing about to get to the hospital.

I drove my mother to the hospital and in the car on that drive, the day before they declared my intubated father dead, I had another of those experiences. Listen deeply, as I describe…

Mother was sitting in the passenger's seat as we drove down a major highway in Los Angeles. Suddenly, that feeling of ecstasy overcame me and the highway was as wide as it was long.

Like I mean *"wiiiiiiiiiiiiiiiiiiiiiiiiiiiiiiiiiiide"* as though it had no end in either direction. It was the freakiest thing ever. All while I'm seeing this, I'm overcome by a sense of utter well-being and magnificent inner strength like never before.

Of course, I said nothing to Mom about what I was experiencing as she was deeply in her own despair and I wanted to be there for her. When we got to the hospital, the entire family gathered to determine whether to remove Dad from the intubation.

My ex, as a physician, knew what was next. I knew we were already there, because I had felt Dad's transition earlier that day, but still couldn't accept it at the time. I remember being comforted by my father's little sister. It was a difficult passage for all of us.

When I returned to Chicago after Dad's funeral, I knew I had the strength to leave Lucifer. Little did I know, nor could I imagine, what was to follow.

Father, Richard King and Jeanne King 1973

# CHAPTER EIGHT

## *My Turning Point*

Four months prior to my father's passing, I was on top of the world. I had three healthy children whom I loved more than life. They were my life, as I think of it.

My clinical practice was booming, and I had just launched a new office constructed and designed for success. I was so proud.

Lucifer and I were in manipulated and inauthentic therapy for abuse. I knew he was feeding the therapist patients, but hadn't realized the extent of it at that time. Actually, I thought things were getting better, until…the straw that broke the camel's back.

**Straw That Broke the Camel's Back**

My oldest son, age 10 at the time, and Lucifer were arguing about what the child should wear to Temple. It was Indian Summer, and our son wanted to wear a short-sleeve shirt, while his father demanded that he wear a long-sleeve shirt. Their dispute quickly cascaded into a violent belt beating with the buckle end of the belt against this child's groin, leaving 10-inch welts.

I got between our son and that belt, insisting that Lucifer pull back from this violence. It sickened me that he beat that child over a personal power struggle. It was, indeed, the straw that broke the camel's back. I couldn't take anymore, after the ten-year history of recurring domestic violence to myself and to our three children.

Foolishly, I thought the system would help us end this dangerous and destructive pattern in our home. The appropriate arrest and abuse charges against Lucifer, along with supervised visitation, were put into place; however, it was the start of another nightmare.

## Legal Domestic Abuse

Lucifer was on a mission to save face and get even. He sought to eliminate Mommy. After four years of legal stalking in which nothing was litigated, attorneys metered roughly $1,600,000 in legal fees, exceeding the reported value of our marital estate. It was an insane "legal" feeding frenzy.

Lucifer had no standing to legally fight for custody, with his court-documented spousal and child abuse findings, so he had to eliminate me by discrediting me. The only way to do that was to back me into a fraudulent criminal charge or an unwarranted psychiatric incarceration.

As a psychologist, I knew where that was going. If I had fallen prey to his antics to have me locked up, I could have been a mental and physical vegetable today, without the means to support myself.

56

Fortunately, as noted by an attorney friend of mine, I had the cogency to recognize their ploy before I had no other options.

After an exhaustive four-year battle, I fled the jurisdiction of the court controlled by a compromised judge. Under normal circumstances, this judge should have recused himself due to obvious bias, but he refused. His wife worked at the same hospital (of mandated reporters) where I had been bringing our oldest son to for child abuse bodily injuries. As you might notice, the political corruption in this case was both apparent and complex.

### From Victim to Survivor to Thriver

Rather than let my losses destroy me, I sought out to leverage my open schedule to heal and become the best version of myself.

While the next handful of years were really difficult, I threw myself into Sedona's healing energy.

Five years later, an attorney (and domestic abuse survivor) and I envisioned Partners in Prevention. The organization was originally set up to bridge healthcare delivery and domestic abuse victim advocacy. I became a sought-after psychologist helping women entrapped in the horror I had just lived.

*"Abuse is about control.*
*When the perpetrator believes*
*he/she is losing their grip,*
*violence will escalate*
*so as to re-establish their control."*

# CHAPTER NINE

## Meditative Writing

*"If everything around seems dark,
look again, you may be the light."*
Rumi

Now I'm going to do one of the most fun things: I'm going to write about writing. As I mentioned earlier, I was a student of language practically all of my life. Latin was the pillar I stood upon. Back in the day, I could translate Latin passages into

English faster than my classmates could read them in English.

I had a mastery of language. It wasn't even that I was good at grammar or language. It was that I loved the resonance of the spoken word and the focus of stepping into the felt meaning that words convey. That was, and is, my skill.

People used to tell me: I bring the heart out in my words. Others would say, you have a way of helping people connect their affect (emotional state) with their intellect though language. Whatever it is, the bottom line is I love "effortless writing," as I so affectionately call it.

## Writing and Healing

This was most profoundly revealed to me when I wrote *All But My Soul*. I wrote the first draft of the narrative of that 440-page personal documentary in 100 days. And the wild part about it was how doing this made me feel—how it left me feeling.

I was writing about the most painful part of my entire life; yet in doing this, I was as high as a kite. I know this sounds ridiculous, but that's how it was for me.

I recall days going to the keyboard upon awakening and looking up hours later well into the day saying to myself, *"Did you meditate, today?"*

Fact is I hadn't left the keyboard. The clarity within me was beyond words. The writing was a meditation. It was a meditation in action. Oh yes, indeed, there were some difficult parts; but the creative flow was pure delight from the inside out.

I had a dear friend Mary who sat with me doing psychological inquiry (The Work by

Bryon Katie) before I wrote each chapter. Then, I'd wake up the next morning and the clarity of it all sprung out of me. And when I'd read what I had written, I couldn't believe it came from me.

Now the best part of writing is how you feel when you walk away from the keyboard after a few thousand words pour out of you. I don't know how it is for other people, but for me it is an uplifting experience like none other.

Then to meditate on top of that takes you to another realm. It's a stillness and quietude so deep; I'd like to say it's magical. I can recall days of running through my house in Sedona, practically naked (it was hot in Sedona) dancing between passages I had written.

It's as though writing carries out the trauma housed in the body in ways that are truly transformational. So, when people say "journal your trauma," trust there is really something to that. It's profound!

What I realized, at some point in this writing journey, is that I had been writing to attorneys all along during the divorce proceedings from 1995-1999. Of course, nothing I wrote changed anything, except it was changing me. Without that writing, I probably would have deteriorated, as so many people do in the circumstances I lived.

**Articles By Dr. King**

In 2007, I made the decision to make a living online. Having already established an expertise in the dynamics of family violence, I set out to write an article a day to educate people suffering in these dysfunctional relationships.

After many months of writing, a dear friend of mine, who was proofreading my articles said, "You have enough here for an entire book."

She was right. I stopped writing and compiled the material for my first two eBooks: *Identifying Domestic Abuse* and *Breaking the Cycle.*

Over the next four years, I wrote and published another 10 eBooks on identifying and healing domestic violence and narcissistic abuse. The writing contributed to my well-being during this time in my life in ways unimaginable.

I can remember days when I would write and then meditate or meditate and then write, wherein I became so high, I feared driving. My consciousness was so expanded; all I wanted was to be still and enjoy. The quietude in those days was remarkable. As I think about it, in writing this now, that's what kept me writing.

After *All But My Soul* was published in 2001, I traveled throughout the country promoting it. This led me to professional speaking for the next five years, which I used to dread earlier in my life. However somehow, someway, I caught the bug and grew to love doing keynote speeches. Privately, what I loved even more was writing them.

As I reflect on my experiences of writing throughout my life, there is one thing that is clear to me. Effortless writing is a meditation in action. The TM Sidhi program, particularly the Flying Block, is instruction in meditation in action. Writing is another form of this for me. I used to call it, "me being Picasso." It is my art form. It is my therapy.

*"Effortless writing is divinely driven."*

**All But My Soul: Abuse Beyond Control**
A Personal Documentary 2001
by Dr. Jeanne King, PhD

*"Let the laser stillness*
*of creative flow energize you*
*from the inside out."*

Domestic Abuse Educational eBooks
by Dr. Jeanne King, PhD.

# Being the Light

# CHAPTER TEN

## Healing Highs

*"Fasting blinds the body in order
to open the eyes of your soul."*
Rumi

I left Chicago in 1999, on this very weekend I'm writing today, to avoid being put in a cage. I didn't want to be incarcerated, or institutionalized, and the time had come for me to flee that inevitability.

As I mentioned, Lucifer and his legal team needed to discredit his established court

Abuse Findings and, of course, shut me up. He made it clear he was out to destroy me.

In that "spirit" of eliminating me, a large sack of kerosene—and gasoline—drenched socks, along with cups of free-floating gasoline–kerosene mixture, was found under the driver's seat of my vehicle. I was later told that this kind of incendiary setup could explode on impact if I were in a car accident—even in a moderate collision.

Then, when I learned there was a Body Attachment placed on me because I defaulted on fighting for the house I didn't want, my advisor said, "It's time to get out of state."

And so, I did after fighting a meaningless, endless battle for four years. Nothing had actually been litigated during the four years of divorce proceedings.

It was protracted legal stalking, reeking of corruption aimed at destroying me. Many people called it legal domestic abuse and the kidnapping of minor abused children.

My oldest was nearly 16 at that time. I had hoped he would someday outgrow his father's control relative to me.

## Doctor Heal Thyself

My whole being was calling one word and that was heal. Heal, woman, heal. I knew Sedona to be a place where I could heal and that's where I headed.

Midsummer that first year, I participated in a "point-holding" event which was preceded by a heavy-duty mineral saturation. I had no idea what I was getting into, but I sensed it would cleanse me in ways not yet known.

Lo and behold after a solid week in the prep cleanse for the work to come, I was sitting on the toilet, mind you, and hit with a surprise of a lifetime. Now I don't mean to gross you out, but here's what happened.

I dropped over a foot of solid tar-like rope from my rectum. It really frightened me because I thought I was discharging an organ. I had no idea what was happening to me. All I knew was I dropped a heavy-duty, tar-like rope from my body. Years later, I connected the dots and realized it was mucoid plaque (i.e. decades of harden mucus-like harmful toxins coating the gastrointestinal track, caked in intestinal lining).

On the point-holding table days later, I experienced breast-feeding as though it was happening in the moment. Much trauma grief was expelled from me in these procedures. And the aftermath was both heavy and light at the same time.

Years later, I picked up on intestinal cleansing as a focused method to cleanse and heal. I was inspired to start one day in reaction to dealing with some family of origin, and family of creation, painful conflict in 2011.

My mother's second husband, whom she married after my father's passing, attempted to have her euphonized in the nursing home where they resided. When I intervened, saving her life, he slandered me to my ex and our adult age children.

In response to this, my youngest son (age 22 at the time), told me he couldn't have a relationship with me because *"It would make his father sad."* This is a child who was tied to the hip with me throughout his formative years and continuing through his tenth birthday. This child was carving lines in his chest for every day he couldn't see Mommy.

I vowed to use this as a catalyst to rise above the pain, the loss, and utter insanity, and not define myself by the absurdity of it all. I sought to make myself a better person in spite of and because of it.

I spent five years engaged in the periodic practice of intestinal cleansing, guided and supported by master cleansing experts. The intestinal cleansing coupled with daily meditation was out of sight.

These words capture it:

- profound clarity and energy
- boundlessness beyond words
- plastered stillness
- infinite quietude
- inner peaceful equanimity
- pockets of pleasantness
- exquisite expansive ecstasy

## 100 days of silence

I learned along the way that the impact of cleansing is enhanced when done in silence. And cleansing enables deeper spiritual experience. Over the years, I developed this habit of taking nearly 100 days of silence per year.

I used to say the silence was so thick, you could cut it with a knife. I disappeared into stillness, going about activity for long periods of time. The pleasantness of that profound quietude is beyond words.

Clearly the meditations augmented the silence and the silence enhanced the meditation. Together they enabled profound states of rest conducive to cleansing and purification.

*"The magic of silence
is not only in the silence
but also, in the afterglow that lingers
days on end after the silence."*

*"Why silence?
So, you may stumble upon bouts
of unadulterated well-being…
And over time acquire the capacity
to sustain it."*

# CHAPTER ELEVEN

# My Mother's Passing

*"You are not a drop in the ocean.*
*You are the entire ocean in a drop."*
Rumi

These were tough years for me, because I was dealing with my mother Audree being exploited by a "care-taker" in a high-end nursing home. It became increasingly more difficult between 2014 through the year following her passing.

Mom was a striking woman in appearance, always with a book in hand. It was her mental escape and the blanket of intellect she wore day in and day out. If it wasn't a book companion, there was knitting needles and yarn neatly tucked in some high-fashioned tote bag next to her side.

She had both a privileged and difficult life, all in one. And she taught me lessons over the years that have molded the very essence of the person I am today.

As a young child, I recall asking her, "Where is God?"

Each time, my dear mother replied with the same answer, which as a child meant absolutely nothing to me.

"God is everywhere," she would say as though she knew.

I would reply, "Well if He is everywhere, why can't I see Him?"

And she would say, "Feel Him."

**God Is Everywhere**

In her passing, she showed me that God is everywhere.

Breathe with me and hear me fully, as I cut and paste exactly what I wrote shortly after she made her transition.

> Then, days later on 12/15/17 Friday (the day she was cremated), I felt Audree in the grocery store the entire time I was there…

> I so distinctly felt her in Wholefoods on College Avenue in Fort Collins, Colorado, late afternoon.

It was the most amazing experience
to feel her presence with me,
**both around me and inside of me.**
**I could smell, sense and feel her.**

She was truly **EVERYWHERE**
…in every crevice of that store.

It was a profound sense of
**contentment** and **utter connection**
with her.

**She was around and within me,**
**and I was her at the same time.**

It was ever so satisfying…
utterly magnificent.

It felt so special to be with it,
as such. It was the absolute most
**profound sense of worthiness** one
might contain.

I remember not wanting it to go, and
wanting to see/feel/experience her
there again.

As I reflect on this again and again, I'm keenly aware of what people mean when they say, **"There is no death."** It's distinctly clear to me that when you die…when you pass, your body stops and your spirit infiltrates the ethers.

You go from individuation to being everywhere. You go from a being incarnated in a body to being everything. You are the Divinity that abounds within and beyond.

And here is the bonus prize: You can influence your presence being known or not by those who remain, as my mother has been doing with me to this day.

*God is everywhere, everyone and everything.*

Thank you, Audree, for giving me the most precious knowing, which will invariably support me for the rest of my life.

## Healing in My Parents' Passing

For many years, I grieved the loss of my parents as I had become accustomed to them in my earthly life. I am seeing, as I write this today, that the passage of each of them helped me process and resolve huge psychological conflict with respect to my family of creation.

My father's passing gave me the strength to no longer enable domestic violence in my home. My mother's passing equipped me with letting go of the emotional heartache around the long-standing consequences of legal domestic abuse.

Together, they gave me strength and peace, which cleared a pathway for enrichment beyond my imagination.

*"When you feel the whispering presence*
*of loved ones who have passed,*
*you know from the core of your being*
*that God is everywhere and everything."*

Mother, Audree King and Jeanne King 2014

Mom and Dad

# CHAPTER TWELVE

## Expanded Awareness

*Love is when God says,*
*"I have created everything for you."*
*And you say,*
*"I have left everything for you."*
Rumi

Clear aspects of the experience my mother showed me in her passing remained with me in a tangible way daily for nearly two months following.

Now, if you thought that was weird, hold on as we take this next step together. If I heard someone telling me what I'm about to tell you, I probably wouldn't believe it. So, please bear with me as you stretch your imagination while I tell you what happened next.

## Expanded Consciousness

In the days, weeks and months that followed my mother's passing, I grew to know my consciousness beyond my physical body. Now I know on face value that sounds ridiculous. Let me explain.

Upon awakening in the morning daily, I walked around my home and could feel my presence—my consciousness—extending outward about a foot beyond my physical body. I was aware of the energetic field around my body. And it was glorious.

After meditation, this awareness was even more present. I distinctly remember the invincibility of it…the clarity in it…the lovingness of it… It was pure lightness of being and interconnectedness of all. It was magical…meaningful and memorable.

This experience remained with me until February 2018, when I started getting pestered, and pressured, by the grand-children to distribute my mother's estate before closing it. My interactions with them led to the dismantling of that magical feeling.

What did remain, however, was the ability to call upon and feel a connection that is beyond my capacity to describe at this point in time.

**Cosmic Consciousness**

I hesitate to even title this section as such, but let's face it, I think we are already here. In proofreading this book, I'm reminded of the innocence I brough to each and every one of these peak experiences described throughout this manuscript.

I didn't have any reference for the experiences I encountered, other than a faint memory of the Maharishi speaking of cosmic consciousness (CC) back in the 70s. All I remember is he used to say after 30 years of meditating one may encounter CC, as we called it. It sounded glorious at the time, but was really just far out gibberish to me back then.

What I'm aware of now is I have been having these experience for the last few decades of my life. I'm keenly aware of my experience of expanded consciousness, the interconnected-ness of all, the connection with that which is larger than me and of which I am a part of, the presence of God and the eternity of one's essence, one's soul. The serenity, the invincibility, the creativity, the joy and the ecstasy in this is truly beyond words.

## Life Pleasures

While I have certainly had my fair share of marvelous moments, I must say the juice that carries one through life is in the moment-to-moment pockets of pleasantness throughout the day. It's in that awareness of being well, being whole and being happy that make for success in life.

It's the little things we do and say to ourselves and to one another. It's the simple aspects of one's experience that are filled with a lightness of being. It's in all of this that we know we are living well.

May the stories and lessons in this little book contribute to your evolution in becoming the happiest, healthiest best version of yourself.

# Being the Light

# PART TWO

## Practical Aspects of Meditation
*Supporting Your Journey*

# Being the Light

# Introduction

The following chapters are excerpted articles I have shared with readers who ask me how to meditate, how to get "me time," how to dial it down and regroup, and how to heal from within. There are as many ways of asking for this renewal and restoration as there are people asking.

1) The first chapter speaks to the core essence of effortless attention in mini-meditations and between sleep and activity.

2) The second chapter outlines in detail the specifics of a daily meditation practice. It deepens the protocol for establishing and maintaining meditative attention.

3) The third chapter addresses coming out of meditation to ensure comfortable carryover into activity.

After reading each chapter thoroughly, set it down and practice as you recall from your reading. Then re-read each of these three chapters again to confirm for yourself that your meditation practice aligns with the basic instruction.

For personal help in learning to meditate, you can contact me at www.InnerSanctuaryOnline.org.

### *On Meditation*

*"There is an ecstasy within and palpable pleasantness after, along with pristine clarity, optimism, well-being and out right happiness.*

*You get there though the silence and stillness. It envelops you and brings you into all of it.*

*Once there, you don't force yourself to meditate. No, no, no, you can't imagine life without meditation."*

Being the Light

# CHAPTER THIRTEEN

## Me Time

### How to Meditate

I hear people in all walks of life express their longing for "me time." The first thought that comes to me is: what better way to hang with me and know my Self than to linger in meditation.

However, for most people, the concept is foreign or something only others do. There is usually an excuse for how they have not been able to allow this privilege for, and with, themselves.

If a trauma patient appears open to the concept of discovering equanimity and renewal in silence, I introduce basic meditation instruction. Some employ this guidance eagerly, and some don't.

If you are one of those people who would meditate if you simply knew how, this writing is for you. Let's start by making meditation easy.

## How to Meditate

We all have the experience of awakening in the morning as long as we are fortunate to be blessed with another day. There is a space between sleep and wakefulness in which you are fully relaxed in body and yet aware of your being awake. That's the magical moment (AKA the hypnopompic state: the state between sleep and full awakening).

In the spirit of introductory ease, simply widen this gap. Linger in the restive bodily experience and **allow the mind to simply be awake unto itself**. If you're asking, "What then do I pay attention to?" stay with me.

You pay attention to attention itself. Let the mind go wherever it is drawn effortlessly. If you find that you are running with thoughts—with active intention versus effortlessly observing—then gently and easily bring your attention back to the restive bodily state that is there upon awakening.

The key words here are **effortlessly and easily**. You are simply guiding the attention back to the bodily felt sense of ease within.

For some people, it may be easier to let the attention find the breath; for others, it may be more natural to be mindful of the full volume of space under the skin. And for those formally trained in mantra meditation, it may be most natural to allow the attention to fall onto the mantra… hearing it over and over in the mind's eye…easily, comfortably and effortlessly.

At some point, there will be a readiness to emerge into activity. This, of course, is a function of how long you have committed to the "discipline" and what the body needs upon awakening.

Whatever that time is for you, make sure that you emerge gently. By that, I mean slowly, gradually, as though you are allowing the dawn to reveal itself within bit by tiny bit.

## Habits of Meditation

Some people will maintain a routine wherein they find these magical moments in their day, and others will return to meditation when reminded. Know this: the glory of this practice is truly in the practice.

This is your "me time." This is the place where you know you are not your thoughts. You are not your emotions. You are not your body.

**You are the larger consciousness within and beyond the boundaries of your experience.**

*"Widen the time*
*between sleep and wakefulness,*
*and you will discover an ocean*
*of bliss before, and within, you."*

# CHAPTER FOURTEEN

## *Meditation for Life*

### *Knowing Your SELF through the Silence Within*

Most people can easily do the practice
described because everyone alive
wakes up. Once you have acquainted yourself
with this exquisite space of eternal
equanimity between sleep and activity, you
may want to experiment with a more formal
routine of meditation practice.

## Setting the Stage for Meditation

Traditionally, meditation is practiced after awakening as part of one's early morning routine. Many meditation teachers will advise that you take care of your bodily needs of elimination in preparation for meditation. Some people may enjoy a light warm beverage before beginning their practice. Generally, one would then find themselves sitting on a cushion or seated comfortably in an upright chair.

No matter where or how you choose to sit, the important thing is to ensure that your head, neck and spine are in a straight vertical line. By this, I do not mean unnatural, stiff or uncomfortably erect. Rather, you want to feel aligned in an upright fashion such that your shoulders are directly in line with (that is, over) your hips, and your pelvis is tilted forward.

Sitting in this fashion allows for you to have a full diaphragmatic breath. As you settle in this position, wearing comfortable clothing, you will more easily remain comfortably still for an extended period of time.

It is also important that you craft the environment such that you are not likely to be disturbed. That could involve silencing your phone and minimizing external distractions or demands for your attention.

**Settling into Meditation**

For over 25 years, I taught meditation to every single patient I worked with as it was the core offering of my biofeedback and stress reduction practice. So, as I share this with you, I'm utterly nostalgic.

Some of the core instruction on how to attend is in the previous chapter. For the sake of clarity and thoroughness, I will elaborate below.

Begin your meditation practice by simply being still within yourself. You may first be aware of the environment around you: the temperature of the room; the sounds in your environment; the feeling of you sitting as you are in the moment.

Then, as naturally inclined, let the attention fall inward toward your inner environment. Be aware of the sensations within, the mood of the moment and the thoughts you are having that come and go.

As you are comfortably ready to do so, allow the attention to find your breath. Without changing the way you're breathing, just simply notice how the breath moves through you and escapes from you effortlessly…as though it breathes you.

You may even want to think the thought, *"It breathes me."* This is a classic Autogenic Phrase that I shared with my biofeedback patients for decades.

### Refinement of Your Attention

With the passage of time, the attention becomes more subtle and your awareness more pristine. In keeping with this, let the attention notice some predetermined object of focus. This might be the sound, sensation or frequency of a mantra, the breath itself, or some sound within your environment.

Note the object of your attention is nothing more than a resting point for your awareness. It is the place you return to again and again as the attention wanders, which it will.

Each time you find yourself actively engaged in directed intentional thought, let that be a signal to remind you to return to your predetermined point of focus…easily, effortlessly, casually and comfortably.

Some will want to maintain this practice for fifteen to twenty minutes. Those more advanced in their practice may choose to sit in meditation for forty minutes. When the time is up, let the focal point fade into the background. And then, notice what remains …and how you feel.

In the golden silence, allow yourself to rejoice in the well-being of the stillness within. Give yourself whatever time you desire to emerge slowly, as you bring your awareness back to activity.

*"Suddenly 'it' tiptoes in and you find yourself observing your thoughts, the mood of the moment and your bodily sensations.*
*It occurs to you that you are not that; rather,*
***you are the full essence of all that is.***
*Enjoy!"*

# Being the Light

# CHAPTER FIFTEEN

## Meditation Carryover

### Happy, Healthy & Whole

As I was ushering in the new year, a dear friend asked me what were my goals for the upcoming year. In years past, I would have thrown loads of visions and plans at that question.

This year, however, the only truly authentic thing that came to me was: be happy, healthy and whole. It's my birthday, and I'm

honoring it in a home spa this weekend.
That's code for extended silence in my world.

As I was coming out of an extremely deep
restorative meditation today, it occurred to
me how lovely it is that I am able to allow this
well-being to spill over into my activity.
There's an ambient glow in activity that
happens when you meditate regularly. The
first few minutes of it, as you emerge into
activity, can be delicate.

That carryover into activity is where the
integration occurs. It's an essential part of the
meditation practice. Without it, the stress
release that happens in the meditation is
truncated and can sit with you like an
unwanted load on your back.

**Where Happy Is Silenced and Shamed**

As I was raising children, I'd take this glow and share it with them in playful glee—from singing to dancing to whatever was before us. Except when their father was around, the well-being in the air was far too often shattered with horrific, verbal and emotional psychological abuse.

I was told how selfish I was to have taken this time to myself. And then there was the ole crazy weirdo verbal bashing. He convinced himself and anyone in an earshot that I was a true "nut" for bathing in the bliss of silence within.

You can't imagine what this did to me. I liken it to a warm cozy nourishing oil massage topped off with an abrasive cold arsenic substance head-to-toe. Now mind you, this was the routine. It was a nightmare living like that. At the time, that's what I thought was the easy part of the narcissistic domestic abuse we lived.

The physical abuse and bodily injury to myself and to our son was the more difficult part of that lifestyle. Now that I see it all from this vantage point, I'm keenly aware of how damaging the mediation bashing was to me.

**Happy, Healthy and Whole**

I'm ever so aware of how blessed I am that I can enjoy health, happiness and wholeness wholeheartedly. Since leaving that tyrannical relationship abuse and letting go of its remnants, I am mindful of the blessings my life affords. So, in answer to the question, what are your goals: mine are to remain happy, healthy and whole. May these goals be yours to enjoy, as well.

Now back to meditation carryover, the key take away is: don't truncate your experience with negativity from yourself or from another. Instead, do something soothing, or neutral, for the first 5 to 10 minutes after surfacing from meditation.

**The way you come out of the meditation determines what you get out of the meditation.**

Whether you are experimenting with a taste of stillness between sleep and wakefulness or establishing a more formal sitting practice of meditation, hold reverence for the carryover into activity. There is a magnificence in utter stillness amidst dynamic activity. Let it be yours to enjoy all the days of your life.

*"The rapture of pleasantness in activity
is the outcome of meditation.*

*Don't judge your experience while in
meditation, look to how you feel in
activity."*

# Epilogue

## Making My Words Yours

I've shared much with you about my relationship with meditation, including how I discovered it and how it discovered me. We delved into how it became such a significant part of both my personal, academic and professional life. Throughout my journey, this routine practice opened me up to profound peak experiences, expanded consciousness in activity, and revelations regarding life, death and the interconnectedness of all.

You have heard me use language to describe altered states of consciousness in and out of meditation. Some of my rhetoric you may connect with and some may seem vague and a bit out there.

Trust me, I understand. If I had not been a student of meditation, all these descriptions of bliss and boundlessness and ecstasy would likely have just been pretty words to me. In case you are not familiar with these experiences in your own life, I'm going to share some everyday phenomenon common to many people that helps them in understanding the experience of meditative altered states of consciousness.

## On the Beach

Most of us have had the fortune of sunbathing at the beach. There is often a losing of oneself in the baking radiant sun. You feel expanded as though your being exists beyond your skin. Stay with me now because this can be similar to the experience of *"expanded-ness"* I have been telling you about that occurs in meditation.

## In Your Hammock

Many people know the same feeling while lying in a hammock. They lose themselves in the gentle swing of the hammock. For some, there can be a loss of awareness of all other things except for the sensation of freely floating. Then, there are moments when your awareness includes all there is as though it is one.

## Sunrises and Sunsets

Now for all of us who have the great fortune of being here now, we can take in either or both sunrise or sunset. In these moments, many people lose themselves in the beauty of it all. While the expanded boundlessness may not be part of this experience, one may feel an enrichment beyond words.

## Baby Glee

The love of a child and interaction with a baby can bring one to states of peak joy. If you have given birth or been a party to one, you know how one can go from excruciating pain to utter contentment when that life is brought into the world.

## During Orgasm

Of all the common experiences people have, I believe an orgasm can most closely be a way to describe that boundlessness you have been hearing me describe.

You know, as well as I, that an experience can go beyond any words you may have to describe it. In fact, this is how I started this book with you. I reminded you that I was going to talk about something that is truly beyond words.

## Psychedelics

I'm saving this for last because I don't have
the words for this that many people use to
draw parallels. As I mentioned earlier, I've
never tried psychedelic or any form of
hallucinogenic drugs, so I'm without words.
But the descriptions I hear of other people's
experiences offer a bridge for describing
altered states of consciousness.

## In Closure

Now do be mindful that the experience of
expanded consciousness is felt as a gradient.
It can be a subtle pocket of pleasantness to a
delicious state of well-being to absolute
unadulterated, profound ecstasy of the
highest order.

Meditation, too, will be filled with ordinary
streams of thought, physical sensations,

moving emotion, pockets of silence, suspension in heightened states of consciousness—from subtle to sensational. It covers the full gamut.

Most important is that you not look for any particular experience, whatsoever. Remember this is an exercise in "just being." Whatever opens up to you in this sacred space is yours to enjoy.

May these chapters inspire you toward your own personal practice of meditating. And if you are meditating, may *Being the Light* deepen your understanding of meditation and the exquisite being you are.

I wish you profound peace, happiness and well-being all the days of your life.

Blessings, Dr. Jeanne King, PhD.

Dr. Jeanne King, Ph.D.

*"It dcesn't matter if you are gripped
for two hours, 20 minutes
or merely having a two-minute taste,
so lcng as you drink from the well
of well-being every day."*

# Life Lessons

In closing, I leave you with three profound life lessons…

- Never hesitate when God speaks to you.

- What you focus on comes your way, no matter what.

- Happiness is within.

# Appendix

## Dr. King's Insights

The following quotes came to me either in meditation, in the quiet moments in my day, or in the context of providing psychotherapy and domestic abuse trauma recovery with patients over many decades.

The quotes in the category **Meditation and Spirituality** sprang from me while meditating. These words express my experience most closely, describing how it feels and what it reveals.

The quotes in the category **Psychology and Trauma Healing** are insights I realized in my personal awakening, and in working with psychotherapy patients suffering in and from domestic abuse dynamics.

These insights have enriched my life, and the lives of my patients and meditation students. Each quote offers invaluable life perspectives, and meditation tips and reflections— supporting well-being. My hope is that they do the same for you.

# Meditation and Spirituality

## Quotes by
## Dr. Jeanne King, Ph.D.

"Meditation is not about doing something. Rather, it's about being nothing to being all that is."

"You don't meditate. Rather, meditation does you. It suddenly tiptoes in, and you find yourself enveloped in it."

"There is nothing better than the silent Temple from within.
Know thyself."

"In the silence, you hear God speak."

"Suddenly 'it' reveals itself, and you find yourself observing your thoughts, the mood of the moment and your bodily sensations. It occurs to you that you are not that; rather, you are the full essence of all that is. Enjoy!"

"You don't seek to find it. Rather, you allow it to find you."

"Sometimes it will be busy with streams of thought you observe and other times you will merely linger in total still silence. Enjoy it all."

"Your rolling stream of thought is part of the meditation. It's not interfering with the meditation; it is the meditation."

"When the silence within fills every morsel of space within and around you, heal and enjoy."

"There is no greater and more satisfying skill to cultivate than your capacity to be in the silent stillness within."

"It doesn't matter if you are gripped for two hours, 20 minutes or merely having a two-minute taste, so long as you drink from the well of well-being every day."

"The rapture of pleasantness in activity is the outcome of meditation. Don't judge your experience while in meditation, look to how you feel in activity."

"Health, happiness and wholeness
are within, so just unhinge and go
deep. It will amaze you."

"When your head opens up and the
blissful boundlessness plasters you in
infinite stillness… you are at one with
all that is. Enjoy."

"When the pleasantness within you
overcomes you, you are home.
Enjoy."

"When you catch yourself smiling
ear-to-ear and feel that inner glow,
that's all that matters."

"Widen the time between sleep and
wakefulness, and you will discover
an ocean of bliss before, and
within, you."

"Find your way into the well of well-being within."

"In the quiet moments between your thoughts, your body reveals its self-repair mechanisms. Be still and learn to heal within."

"When expansive silence plasters you into utter stillness, nothing else is wanted or needed."

"When the silence bursts into ecstasy, you are home."

"When your inner space becomes your outer space and all is one, you are home."

"When the stillness within wraps you in a blanket of blissful love…"

"When you dwell in the expansiveness of who you really are, it becomes
apparent that your body is a cast, and
your sense organs are simply the
boundaries of your experience."

"When you close your eyes and
within moments find yourself in utter
boundless silent stillness, you know
you are home."

"The magic of silence is not only in
the silence but also in the afterglow
that lingers days on end after the
silence."

"On or about the fourth day of
silence, the inner bliss emanates out
and surrounds you in a blanket of
love and grace."

"From the silence comes the purest thought and the wisest wisdom."

"Both your options and answers dwell in the quiet moments between your thoughts."

"Once the silent stillness tiptoes in, you feel as though you are hugging God and God is hugging you. It is the most nourishing experience ever."

"When the stillness within holds you in a place of infinite love…"

"You are not your thoughts, feelings or sensations.

You are the consciousness beyond that… discoverable in silent stillness."

"There is nothing that surpasses the peace within."

"If you can taste the sweet bliss of silence within, you can endure anything."

"Melting in the meaningful moments of meditation gives perspective to all other things."

"You get to choose how you're going to ride this wave. I say, 'tuck and flex.' And always know you can access well-being from within."

"Bathing in peace are words that try to express the glory of sitting in meditation."

"To simply close your eyes and feel
the most compelling peace within is
the greatest joy to behold."

"What an extraordinary precious
gift to simply close your eyes and
experience heaven on earth.
Learn to meditate."

"The greatest gift you can give
yourself is a dip into the silent steady
stillness within."

"When you emerge from meditation
and the first thought you have is: 'It
doesn't get better than that,' you
know you are into something good."

"When stillness envelops you from
within, boundlessness abounds."

"It doesn't matter how you get there as long as you do. Find the peace within and you will burst with delight beyond your imagination."

"In and through the stillness and silence is you experiencing everything, simultaneously. And through which… you recalibrate, nourish and harmonize.

It's truly a setting aside of ego and just being. And allowing the enjoyment of that. It's healing, purifying and fun."

"Silence for me is essentially sustaining an expanded awareness …sustained meditation in action."

"The quieter you get, the more the silence becomes a palpable stillness on the outside and within."

"The stillness can be so dense. It extends out of your skull making your head feel four times its size."

"Listen gently in the quiet moments between your thoughts. That's where your truth resides."

"Know your power in the stillness between your thoughts, and you will know true empowerment."

"There is a point at which the vibrancy of silence fills all the space. And therein, healing happens effortlessly."

"Everything we seek is already here
in the space between our thoughts."

"Bask in your boundlessness and
drink from the well of well-being
daily."

"When you cleanse your body,
you open your heart to the
Divinity within."

"When you exercise free will,
you are paying homage to God."

"When you close your eyes and the
universe opens up onto its infinite
wisdom, you are home."

"Divinity abounds and awaits to be
let in."

"The Divinity that abounds whispers saliently in the silence within you."

"Awaken to the fact that we are all infinite beings. There is no death; only a refocusing of attention and a redistribution of energy.

Rejoice in the splendor of your beingness and the fact that we are here now."

"When you die, your body stops and you infiltrate the ethers. You go from individuation to being everywhere. You go from being incarnated in a body to being everywhere. You emerge with all that is.

…And you can influence your presence being known by those living or not."

"For some people, prayer is speaking to God, whereas meditation is listening to God."

"When you feel the whispering presence of loved ones who have passed, you know from the core of your being that God is everywhere and everything."

"When you are filled with the love of God, you naturally love others."

"When splendor shows up in meditation, it's not because you created it. Rather, it's because you created the requisite conditions for it to reveal.

…Hence the term self-revelation. Enjoy!"

"Why silence? So, you may stumble upon bouts of unadulterated well-being... And over time acquire the capacity to sustain it."

"Meditative silence feels like your skull is wide open, and every morsel of your being is in communion with all that is.

When you emerge back into activity, there is a blanket of peace, calm equanimity within and around you."

"Whether one calls it 'through the veil,' or 'in the vortex' or 'being loving awareness,' once you find your way into the stillness within, you will open to infinite resources."

Dr. Jeanne King, Ph.D. 2024

# Psychology and Trauma Healing

## Quotes by
### Dr. Jeanne King, Ph.D.

"The day you awaken to the fact that your well-being has nothing to do with anything anyone says or does is the day you set yourself free."

"You make a conscious decision to be happy, healthy and whole. And then you eliminate experiences that take you away from that."

"When you truly care about yourself, you say 'no' to people who don't."

"Inner strength is knowing your
healing essence from the inside out."

"When your worthiness has nothing
to do with what others think of you,
you are free."

"Worthiness is a given and well-
being is within."

"The natural state is happy."

"You have one job in life.
Be happy."

"What you focus on expands, and
the more you focus on it, the more of
it you bring upon yourself. Choose
your focus wisely."

"Change is an inside job."

"In your deepest darkness is your brightest light."

"You can't wait until life is no longer hard to decide to be happy. Be happy now."

"If you have an air of pleasantness about 80% of the time, I'd say you have stabilized being into something good. Enjoy!"

"Only do what honors and nourishes you. And leave behind what's toxic to you.

Everyday become wiser in knowing the difference."

"Conscious eating is truly about letting your food be your medicine and your medicine be your food."

"Don't feed what you don't want to grow; instead, nourish what you seek to flourish.

"You can't push against someone or something and remain in alignment with yourself.

When both people realize this, a significant shift toward individual and relationship harmony naturally occurs."

"The only thing you can really control is your relationship with yourself. So, let go of your pursuit to control your significant other."

146

"When it is time to go, do so quickly and quietly…in peace. It doesn't matter if they understand; you do!"

"When there is no trust and no respect, there is no point in going back and rehashing the details. Move on."

"People often ask, 'When do you let go of a toxic relationship?'

My answer is: When you have had enough. It's a very personal decision."

"If you are a man or a woman estranged from your children through divorce, know this: you are in a controlling abusive relationship. Period."

"You're not going to gain anything by so-called understanding they may get from your communication. If anything, you risk the peace you have gained.

If you are not wanting to continue a relationship you experience as toxic, then moving onward is in your interest. The essential keys are to disengage and dissolve."

"Forgiveness frees oneself, serving the one forgiving."

"No matter what happens to you, you get to choose whether it takes you down or inspires you to be the best version of yourself."

"History is the set of lies that you believe. Uncover truth and you will set yourself free."

"It's easier to fool someone than
it is to convince them that they have
been fooled. One must question their
own thoughts to break a spell."

"When you realize having something,
or some person, in your life costs you
the health and well-being of your life,
letting go becomes practical,
purposeful and productive in
reestablishing your health and
well-being."

"Sustained fear is psychologically
self-imposed."

"Pay attention to what has your
attention and you will suddenly
recognize that you are not what you
are paying attention to."

"When you put Zen thought and practice right smack in the middle of domestic abuse treatment, healing happens."

"Interacting with an abuser is like walking on eggshells. Interacting with an adult child controlled by an abuser is like walking on glass."

"A child who is victimized by 'parental alienation' has one parent that doesn't exist and one parent that doesn't allow the child to exist."

"Living in an abusive relationship is a lot like being wrapped in a boa constrictor."

"You cannot change a domestic abuse offender from being abusive. Only he/she can do that."

"It's not about controlling the growth of other; rather, it's about recognizing the experience you are having and knowing what sustains it. From here, you are liberated in your choices."

"People don't remember what you say and do with them, as much as they remember how they felt during and after their experience with you. Be kind."

"Abuse is about control. When the perpetrator believes he/she is losing their grip, violence will escalate so as to reestablish their control."

"The creepy thing about gaslighting
is that it is often just below the
threshold of awareness, and it gets
under your skin. It distorts reality so
as to confuse the target. Notice."

"When you think your salvation is in
stopping the train, think again. You
will serve yourself better by getting
off the tracks."

"Violence erupts out of vulnerability;
not power."

"If you challenge an establishment,
they will silence you and cover up
what you seek to expose. That's
exactly what happens in
intergenerational domestic violence
families."

"When someone is poisoned against you, they can be toxic to you."

"Fear, greed, manipulation and control versus love, compassion and empathy. Your choice moment-to-moment."

"When we resist something, we must honor that resistance even if we don't understand it in the moment. And trust it will reveal itself at some point."

"You are interacting with an experience within, and either praising other because of it or punishing other for it. Simply notice."

"Bring the wholeness that you are into the lives of others. This is the greatest gift."

"Psychotherapy and psychological healing are fundamentally about helping people access their higher resources and shift their personal perspectives."

"Sometimes fixing it is accepting it; not changing it."

"Psychotherapy is a journey inward that reveals a new path outward."

"It's not what happens to you in life; it's what you do with it that matters most, every time."

"Let the laser stillness of creative flow energize you from the inside out."

"Effortless writing is divinely driven."

"May your feet be firmly placed on the ground, your heart wide open and your mind melting in clarity and ease… all the days of your life."

Being the Light

# Your Personal Notes

Being the Light

# About the Author

D r. Jeanne King, Ph.D. is a clinical psychologist and meditation teacher with over four decades of experience. She has enjoyed the satisfaction of contributing to the psychological healing of people from all walks of life through her compassionate and insightful approach.

Dr. King's life is dedicated to exploring the miracles of meditation and the effects of effortless writing on enhanced well-being. Her natural talent lies in speaking directly to the hearts of her readers through the written word, bringing their innermost experiences forward in a way that fosters deep personal reflection and growth.

She has authored 15 books and over 560 articles on a diverse range of topics, from the psychophysiology of meditation to healing narcissistic domestic abuse trauma.

Dr. King is the founding director of Partners in Prevention, a 501(c)(3) nonprofit dedicated to providing innovative therapeutic interventions and online educational resources, helping individuals and couples heal intimate partner abuse.

Dr. King earned her doctorate in Psychology from Northwestern University and has trained with some of the leading figures in mind body medicine and psychotherapy. She was the founding director of the Chicago Center for the Treatment of Pain and Stress and past president of the Illinois Biofeedback Society. Dr. King pioneered the Biofeedback and Stress Reduction Program, conducted in hospitals with thousands of patients for the treatment of pain, stress and illness.

It is with immense joy that she shares the stories contained in *Being the Light* in this memoir with you. Through these narratives, she invites readers to explore the real transformative power of meditation in their own lives.

For more of Dr. King's writings and resources, visit www.InnerSanctuaryOnline.org

Being the Light

Being the Light

www.ingramcontent.com/pod-product-compliance
Lightning Source LLC
Chambersburg PA
CBHW051622120626
46551CB00014B/1902